Moving Hills of Sand

Moving Hills of Sand

by Julian May
Illustrated by John Hawkinson

Hawthorn Books, Inc.   Publishers   New York

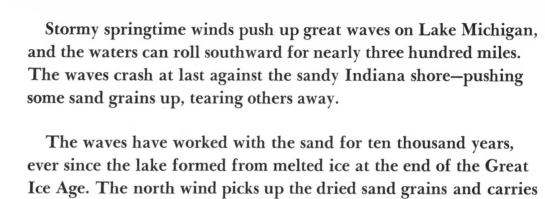

Stormy springtime winds push up great waves on Lake Michigan, and the waters can roll southward for nearly three hundred miles. The waves crash at last against the sandy Indiana shore—pushing some sand grains up, tearing others away.

The waves have worked with the sand for ten thousand years, ever since the lake formed from melted ice at the end of the Great Ice Age. The north wind picks up the dried sand grains and carries them inland, beyond the storm beach where gulls feed on stranded fish, and bobbing shorebirds eat drowned insects.

Where sand meets a barrier and starts to pile up, a dune is born. A little hill grows, its shallow slope pointing into the wind. Sand grains leapfrog their way to the top of the new dune and tumble over the crest, down the steep lee side.

The growing dune may gradually travel inland, pushed by the wind. A moving hill of sand is called a "living" dune, and it may slowly bury shrubs, trees, fences, even houses that stand in its way.

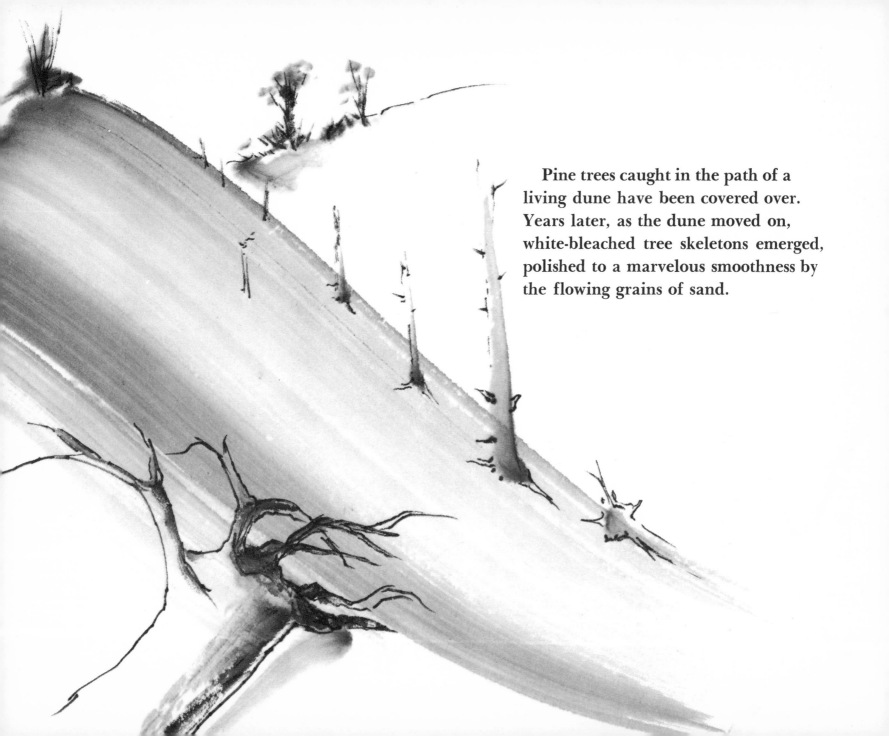

Pine trees caught in the path of a living dune have been covered over. Years later, as the dune moved on, white-bleached tree skeletons emerged, polished to a marvelous smoothness by the flowing grains of sand.

Some kinds of green plants can halt
the movement of a living dune. Among
the first to grow in moving sand is the
marram grass, sharp and tough, with a
deep-growing web of roots that binds
the sand and prevents it from traveling.

The wind brings fluffy seeds of the
cottonwood, which take root and grow
even upon the flanks of a "living" dune.
As the sand engulfs a cottonwood, its
lower branches change into roots and the
tree rises above the sand flood by
sending out new growth.

Behind the partly anchored young dunes, hollows are sometimes filled with shallow water. Here the backswimmers and whirligig beetles swim in company with tadpoles and the larvae of mosquitoes. Sand reeds and horsetails take root in the moist sand, making perching places for dragonflies.

Farther inland, rank after rank of sand hills rears toward the sky. The farther they are from the lake, the more ancient they are. Each row of dunes once marked the shore of the lake, which has grown smaller with passing centuries.

The oldest dunes are completely clothed in green. Forests of beech and maple have tied down the sands that were "living" and moving ten thousand years ago. After the marram grass and cottonwood first bound them, the ancient dunes became home to an everchanging parade of plants and animals.

sand
cherry

beach
pea

cassia

cactus

sand
willow

cross
section

Sand cherries and cassia lived and
died. Prickly pear cactus, beach pea, and
willow grew, and the doodlebug dug its
cone-shaped pits and lay in wait at the
bottom for unwary ants that tumbled in.

Each year, plants and animals lived
and died and their bodies returned to
the earth, enriching it so that new living
things might arise. New plants—pines,
juniper, bunchberry, wild grape—were
able to grow in the improved soil.

The passing of more hundreds of years found the sand even more firmly bound. After the pine forests came groves of black and white oak, with elms and basswood. Squirrels and deer bounded through the hills. The marshes between the dunes were homes for ducks, geese, and herons.

The oaks, shedding their leaves each year, enriched the soil still more. The top layers of sand, which had been nearly white when the dunes were newborn, were now dark with humus—decaying plant matter. Moles tunneled among the tree roots.

Beautiful beeches and maples reared
up among the smaller oaks and sassafras
trees. Ferns and shrubs now carpeted the
slopes of the ancient sand hills. Between
the oldest dunes and the lake lay row
upon row of younger dunes—some
clothed with oak, some clothed with
pine, and the youngest barely covered
with marram grass.

At one time the sand dune country stretched around the entire southern end of Lake Michigan—from what is now Chicago eastward to Michigan City, Indiana. As settlements became villages and villages became cities, the duneland became smaller and smaller.

The wolves and wildcats that had once roamed the dunes were hunted down by men. The Indians who had lived there vanished. Raccoons, opossums, squirrels, rabbits, and deer were fewer but did not disappear entirely.

Great portions of duneland were
swallowed by the spreading cities of
Chicago and Gary. Maple forests became
farms. Summer homes were built along
the lakeshore, cutting the beach into
small fenced sections.

Many people were saddened when it seemed that the dunes wilderness would disappear. It was a place unlike any other in the Midwest—a gentle, wild land where hikers could walk for hours among wooded hills.

Sitting high on top of a shore dune, a person could see for miles.
And between the dunes were great patches of wild blueberries
and mysterious swamps alive with songbirds.

In 1916, it was suggested that the dunelands be made into a National Park. In 1925, one of the loveliest sections of the dunes became a State Park, but the lands on either side lost their beauty as factories and houses spread over them. Groups of nature-lovers continued to try to save what was left of the dunes so that others would be able to enjoy their beauty and peace. Finally, in 1968, money to purchase the Indiana Dunes National Lakeshore was set aside by Congress.

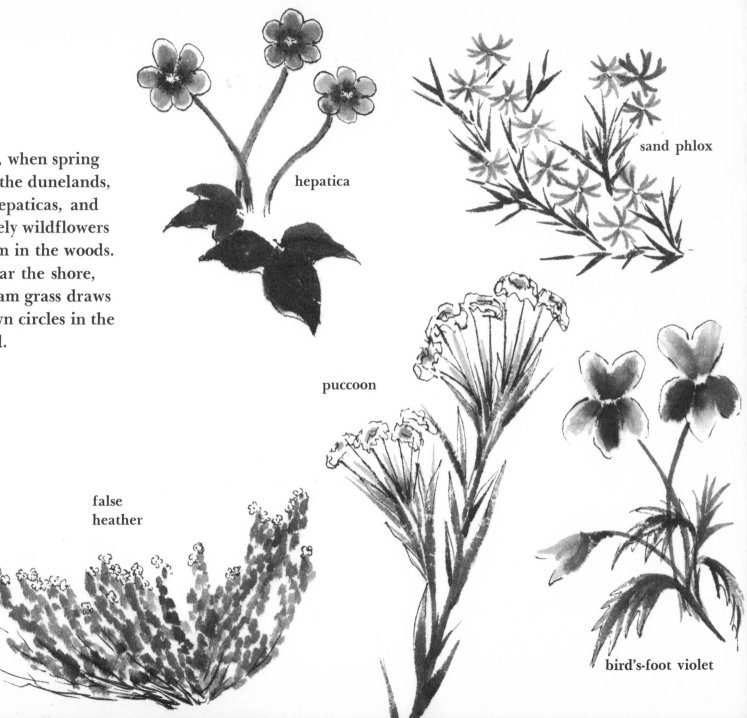

Today, when spring comes to the dunelands, violets, hepaticas, and other lovely wildflowers still bloom in the woods. Down near the shore, the marram grass draws windblown circles in the pale sand.

hepatica

sand phlox

puccoon

false heather

bird's-foot violet

In summer, hikers stand in the center of **Big Blowout**, a graveyard of silver-gray tree skeletons, and then race away from its heat and eery silence to plunge into the cool waters of the lake.

When fall comes to
the sand hills, campers
set up their tents and
trees wear gold and
scarlet costumes. On the
beach, the smoke from
driftwood bonfires
streams away over the
mirror-still lake water.

And finally, winter snow binds the dunes and ice piles in strange shapes offshore. Then the land takes on the look of ten thousand years ago, when Ice-Age glaciers formed the lake and gave birth to the beautiful moving hills of sand.